Teacup • Toy
Dog Training & Care

The Secrets to Raising the Ultimate Purse Baby

by Tinka LaRue

CLADD
PUBLISHING

Cladd Publishing Inc.
USA

This publication is designed to provide accurate information regarding the subject matter covered. It is sold with the understanding that neither the author nor the publisher is providing medical, veterinary, legal, or other professional advice or services. Always seek advice from a competent professional before using any of the information in this book. The author and the publisher specifically disclaim any liability that is incurred from the use or application of the contents of this book.

Teacup • Toy Training & Care: 24 Professional Secrets

ISBN 978-1-946881-00-7 (e-book)
ISBN 978-1-946881-04-5 (paperback)

Contents

Chapter 1: Introduction

EXTRAORDINARY

This book is not your ordinary large breed training manual. Purse baby parents do not purchase their high-priced teacups to keep outside in the backyard, nor to sit in the car while they shop.

BEST FRIENDS

The lust of toting a Teacup or Toy breed around the town or globe is fascinating. There is no limit to the places you can take your little one including grocery stores, parks, theater, shopping centers, airplanes and even restaurants. You and your doggie are about to embark on a friendship that will undoubtedly last a lifetime.

ORDINARY TRAINING METHODS DON'T WORK

Parents of Teacup and Toy breeds need so much more than to train their pooches to pee on the lawn. They need a training program that can teach their doggies how to pee and poo on a pad; whether in their home, friends, or a public restroom at the airport in between flights.

THE SECRETS

Following the information in this book will ensure success in raising a healthy, fun-loving, well minded, and fantastic companion. Teacup and Toy breeds are unique and require a specialized set of training and management methods.

- You will soon be learning how to increase your dog's life expectancy through a powerful diet.
- What supplies are needed for general care.
- Secrets to effectively training and communicating with your dog. The Fast-Track Training instructions make it a breeze.
- Fully housetrain your pooch with a method specifically designed for your dog.
- Types of clothing they will need for health and safety.
- How to baby-proof your entire home.
- Establishing roam-zones.

- Creating a perfect dog that can travel the globe.
- Properly using crates and puppy apartments.
- Learn about the hidden dangers in your home, lawn, food, vaccinations, dog jewelry, collars and plants.
- Holistic remedies for fleas, ticks, spiders, ants, parasites, and tear eyes.

Chapter 2: Learn Their Traits

CUTE

Teacups, Toy, and Micro-Breeds are as cute as a button, and just the right size to fit in your purse or a carrying bag. They weigh next to nothing, which makes these dogs very easy to carry around without causing shoulder pain.

APARTMENT DWELLERS

Due to their small size, they don't need much outdoor exercise. They usually get sufficient exercise running around inside.

GREAT WATCH DOG

They are great at letting their parents know that someone is at the door. Small-breeds tend to be very territorial and loud.

INDOOR POTTY-TRAINING

Teacups and Toy breeds are stubborn when it comes to indoor potty-training. If you give an inch, they will take a mile.

GROOMING

Shedding breeds just need to be bathed and have their nails clipped periodically, and they are good to go. However, non-shedding breeds will require regular visits to the groomer.

TRAVEL COMPANIONS

These little guys make traveling about as easy as it gets. They can make a comfy home in your purse or carry case, and fit comfortably just about anywhere. They don't mind being in small confined spaces. Most Teacup and Toy breeds prefer the confinement. They truly enjoy being with their parents.

FRAGILE

Small-breeds can be easily injured by something as simple as falling off the couch. They may seem agile and strong, but their bones and joints can be severely damaged if allowed to jump off high objects.

LIFE SPAN

They can live anywhere from 5 to 20 years.

HEALTH COMPLICATIONS

These small-breeds, if not cared for properly, could send you digging deep into your pockets for vet bills. Breeders of these tiny dogs have many incentives to keep them ultra-small to fetch more profits.

COLD TEMPERATURES

These are warm weather dog-breeds. If you live in a colder climate, it will be necessary to put warm clothes on your doggie whenever you go outside. Most small-breeds hate cold weather and will do just about anything to avoid it.

ONE PARENT DOGS

They tend to bond to just one parent and will remain loyal to that person. Without proper socialization, Teacup and Toys have been known to nip or bite whenever they feel uncomfortable. It is essential to socialize your Teacup and Toy from an early age to avoid aggression.

Take your doggie where ever you go. When people swoon over how cute they are, pass them around. This will dramatically help form them into a well-rounded, kind natured pooch.

TAKING THE TIME

If you take the time to train and socialize your pooch properly, they make lovely pets. Dress them up in cute outfits, take them anywhere, and you have a best friend for life. So, if you're ready for lots of snuggling, then you and a doggie will be a perfect match!

Chapter 3: Interesting Facts

- The Teacup and Toy breeds are considered a lapdog, companion.
- Teacups got their name because they can fit into a teacup.
- Average litter size is 1-3 puppies, and at the most 6.
- These breeds have more C-sections than any other dog.
- 3 top leading causes of death for the Teacup breeds are - cardiovascular disease, trauma and infection.
- The standard size for an adult should be 7 pounds and under.
- The Teacup is the smallest of all purebred dogs.
- Life expectancy average is 12 years.
- Teacup and Toy breeds make exceptional family pets.
- They generally get along well with cats.
- Teacup and Toys can be found in a vast variety of colors.
- They can suffer from phobias, such as being home alone (separation anxiety) fear of traffic and being afraid of unknown dogs.

- Teacup and Toy breeds are often hyper and very enthusiastic to play.
- They can be light to moderate shedders, or not shed at all.

Small-breeds can become great service dogs. They help with all sorts of tasks, including leading the blind and acting as therapy dogs.

Chapter 4: Must Have Items

Only We Know

I have included in this book real life solutions to fix the problems only parents of small-breeds will encounter. Before I begin discussing the ins and outs of properly caring for and training small breeds, I will need you to start putting together the items listed below.

1. Large square sturdy laundry hamper (a sturdy box will work)
2. Pee pads (a large box)
3. Pee pads holder (optional)

4. High quality food (I use a mixture of dry, canned and a super-food)
5. Sturdy water and food dishes (make sure they are shallow and easy to drink/eat from)
6. Designated safe place area (that is baby proofed and or a large gated area)
7. Safe clothing (no long sleeves for puppies)
8. Harness with neck scoop
9. Retractable leash
10. Hypoallergenic natural baby wipes
11. Hypoallergenic dog bathing soap
12. Sturdy pet purse or carrying case
13. Poo bags
14. Bag of soft tiny treats
15. Baked chicken, steak, lamb (unseasoned and cooled)
16. Natural bone
17. Puppy chew toy or squeaky chew toy

Chapter 5: Baby Proofing

GETTING HURT

It sounds a little funny to baby proof your home for a puppy. However, these little guys are fragile and can easily hurt themselves or be harmed by others. I listed many of the most dangerous and overlooked ways for your new one to get hurt.

1. Block off all stairs (up and down)
2. Create a safe space for your new puppy free from other animals, plants and young children
3. Keep the safe space where they can be easily monitored (can be gated off)
4. Have a clean place for food and water away from bedding
5. Block off areas where the puppy can crawl underneath chairs, recliners, sofa, tables etc.

Chapter 6: Teacup, Toy Care

WARMTH

When you embark on a small-breed, it becomes vital that you help them maintain a comfortable temperature. With that being said, there are some small issues with clothes causing knots in long hair.

If this becomes a problem, you can always opt for a puppy cut or use small bands to tie their hair back. Either way, your new doggie must stay at a comfortable temperature at all times.

NERVOUS

In addition, your new small-breed may come with a variety of nervous issues. They may chew things into bits and pieces, nibble ends of cloth or wood furniture, they may even shake uncontrollably.

In many cases they will, if allowed, itch a whole in themselves. I mean this! If you do not have clothes on this breed the chance of them scratches or nibbling a whole in their skin is very high. This will lead to sores that could easily become infected.

HIGHER PRICES – FOR SMALLER DOGS

Now that we have touched on the topic of breeders and their goal of keeping the dogs small for higher prices; you should be aware of the complications your new puppy will have when brought home.

COMMON HEALTH ISSUES

Teacup and Toy breeds can be healthy with relatively few health problems. They tend to have a long life, often living up to 14 years and beyond.

However, small-breeds commonly suffer from obesity. This is due to overfeeding by their owners. Since your puppy is ultra-small, it is important to remember that they don't require heaping bowls of food. Small-breed dogs that are obese may suffer significantly from inflamed joints.

Progressive Retinal Atrophy. This is a condition affecting the eye. It is when the nerve cells at the back of the eyeball slowly degenerate, which can lead to blindness.

Portosystemic Shunt. This condition is a congenital disability that affects the liver function which can lead to other health problems.

FRAGILE BONES. Teacups and Toys are prone to fractures if they experience physical injury.

TRACHEA COLLAPSE. This condition occures when the rings that form the windpipe the neck become weakened and collapse.

LUXATING PATELLA. This is a condition whereas the kneecap does not fit properly into the groove of the leg bone. This creats painful limping, holding the hind leg out straight and refusal to put weight on the affected leg.

HYPOGLYCEMIA. Your puppy can develope low blood sugar resulting in death. This condition is more common in puppies than adults but can happen at any time regardless of age.

DRY EYE. This condition is when your Yorkie has an insufficient production of fluids in the eye. Many times, this leads to eye irritation, and itchy eyes.

BRONCHITIS. Small-breed dogs are also prone to an inflammation of the lungs which causes coughing and wheezing.

HYPOGLYCEMIA HAPPENS FAST

First is to be aware of the puppies need for regular food and water. Since your puppy is super small, it will need food spread throughout the entire day until they are out of the puppy stage. You will need to have food on hand and watch your puppy like a hawk for any signs of hunger. These breeds can suffer quickly from hypoglycemia (low blood sugar), which causes seizures and death if not carefully monitored

WEIGHT SELECTION

If you have not already brought your puppy home, you could avoid some of these issues by selecting a dog that is larger instead of smaller. Not only will your new puppy be healthier, but also more capable of breeding down the road if that is something you're interested in. If not, that is fine too, just remember that your new puppy should not be left alone for long periods of time for the first six months.

DANGEROUS

Specific clothing styles can become dangerous for your puppy. Since their arms and legs are so small, they can accidently get caught up in the sleeves. It is critical that you choose clothing that is sleeveless and that properly fit. If you go for sleeves or spaghetti straps, you must be aware that your puppy can get twisted up and fall.

Teacup, Toy Development Stages

WHEN DO PUPPIES OPEN THEIR EYES?

Your puppy's eyes will open during the second week of life. A tiny gap appears between the eyelids in the corner of the eye, and you'll see the puppy peeing out through it. Within a few days, the eye will open fully. Sometimes one eye opens faster than the other.

WHEN DO PUPPIES START WALKING?

The third week is all about puppies getting up on their feet. Most puppies are standing and taking their first steps by the end of the third week.

PUPPY SOCIALIZATION STAGES

Puppy socialization is the process that all dogs need to go through to help them live stress free in our world. It's all about learning not to fear new experiences, and to welcome human beings as friends.

The first window for socialization closes around three months old. This is the time when your puppy will most readily accept and adapt to new experiences. During this stage, you will need to take them everywhere and ensure they are exposed to as much of the world as possibly.

The second window comes again as your dog enters its teenage years. During this period between 6-12 months, your young dogs that were fully socialized as puppies may again become fearful and need their socialization program refreshed once more.

How to Socialize Your Puppy:

- Allow each family member to hold, pet, play, handle the toys, and feed snacks.
- Invite family members or friends that visit your home frequently to meet your and handle your pup. Introduce them one by one and allow each person to hold your puppy.
- Allow children of all ages that visit your home to play with your dog and become playmates. Advise them of rules like no ear or tail pulling and no hitting.
- Take your pup for frequent walks in your neighborhood. Allow them to become familiar with other dogs and people by stopping for a moment and chatting up friends.
- Allow your pup to play with others at the dog park. Remove your puppy if you see any unusual or aggressive behavior whether it is the other dogs or your dog.

Let your puppy tag along with you to restaurants, outdoor picnics, park get togethers, BBQs, pet stores, and more.

Chapter 7: Correctly Sizing

CONFUSION

Unfortunately, if you have ordered clothing off the internet before reading this book, you may have a few things to return. There is so much confusion when trying to select a correct size for your precious pooch.

The best way to order any type of clothing or harness is by matching your dog's measurements to the measurements on the items description. You may be dumbfounded to find that in one brand your puppy is an XXS and in another is a Small.

Clothing Sizes Are Unreliable

NO STANDARD

Rule number one for sizing a dog for any apparel or harness is do not rely on the "Size" alone (extra small, small, medium, etc.). There is entirely no standard in the pet industry for sizing. What a medium is to one manufacturer is a small to another.

Getting It Right The 1st Time

EXCITING

Getting ready to purchase your Teacup or Toy's first clothing can be one of the most exciting experiences. It is essential that you get the size right the first time. Many online dog apparel companies do not offer returns. If they are kind enough to do so, you will likely pay for shipping and restocking.

WASTING YOUR MONEY

Let's say that you have found the perfect outfit. The next step is to find the information concerning neck/chest size, mid-section/belly/girth, neck to back length or weight. If the measurements are not clear or missing, then do not bother to waste your time. Look for listings that provide at least two different measurements and or weight. Most errors in purchasing dog apparel items are caused by parents having to guess.

Taking Measurements

MEASURING WORKS BEST IF YOU HAVE A FABRIC RULER

If you don't, take a piece of string or yarn and use it to wrap around the areas you are measuring. Create a mark on the yarn, then use a straight ruler to get the measurements based on yarn length.

FOR CHEST MEASUREMENTS:
Measure around the back of the neck and drop down a little in the front under the chin to encompass the chest.

FOR NECK TO TAIL LENGTH:
Measure the base of the neck to the base of the tail (not the tip of the tail).

FOR THE MID-SECTION/BELLY/GIRTH:
Measure the widest part of their mid-section.

WEIGHT

Place your puppy on an electronic scale or use the weight from the last vet visit (give a few more ounces for growth).

GOING TO THE NEXT SIZE

If your measurement is the maximum of the item, you might want to go up one size, to allow for comfort and weight fluctuation. Remember that most cotton items will shrink slightly in the wash.

BEST SCENARIO

The ideal is to come in under the maximum or fall within the range. Of all the measurements, the weight is the least important. If your dog falls out of the weight range, but all other measurements match up, it will likely fit just fine.

Chapter 8: Necklace Danger

CHOKING HAZARD

I am sure you can imagine how a little mischief puppy can make it their mission to choke on necklace beads, or get their paw caught and rip their little nails. They have also been victims of choking by catching the necklace on something they crawled under. Use a watchful eye when dressing them jewelry.

SAFETY WITH STYLE

By using a designer collar, you can get the posh look of a fancy necklace, while removing the danger that dangling necklaces can pose. However, collars on a small-breed should never to be used for walking.

Chapter 9: Harness vs. Collar

NECK INJURIES

A harness removes the strain off your dog's neck and trachea that a collar will cause. Instead, use a vest-style harness that attaches to a leash.

The harness will evenly distribute the pressure on the chest and belly. Our little dogs can be hurt by the constant pressure on their neck. However, the suffering goes beyond the neck area and causes seemingly unrelated illnesses.

THYROID DAMAGE

Dog that pull on their collar style restraint, tend to have a higher rate of thyroid issues. Many veterinarians speculate that thyroid problems happen when a collar pulls against your dog's thyroid regularly; this trauma eventually leads to inflammation and bruising.

When your dog's thyroid gets inflamed, its immune system sends white blood cells to the area to remove the inflammation. The white blood cells do get rid of the inflammation, but they eventually start to wear down the thyroid. After a while the thyroid becomes damaged.

EAR/EYE DAMAGE

When using a collar style restraint, it restricts the dogs blood flow to its eyes and ears. When blood flow is cut off regularly, it causes swelling, and this swelling damages their eyes and ears over longer periods of time.

Nerve damage

Dog collars can damage the nerves in your dog's front legs. When your dog's nerves are pinched, it causes a tingly feeling in their front paws, and dogs will continuously lick their paws to relieve the ache.

Neck injury

Yanking on a collar style restraint can give your dog whiplash; Do not jerk on the neck with heavy force. Often, dogs don't understand why their leash jerks their neck, so they become frustrated, depressed or aggressive.

The best way to prevent neck, nerve and thyroid damage is to get your dog a top-quality harness.

Chapter 10: Diet Is Everything

LIFE OR DEATH

I cannot stress enough on how a proper diet is an absolute essential for your small-breed. Having the right food can save the life of your new puppy, increase their lifespan, provide a healthy coat and eliminate tearing eyes. The diet will have a tremendous effect on their skin and stave off anxiety itching along with common diseases.

OPTIMAL DIET IS NUMBER ONE

Your Teacup or Toy will likely come with some inherited health issues that have to be addressed and adequately cared for.

1. You want to achieve a healthy poo that is firm and not runny. If they continuously have watery poo, you are not only ruining your carpets and floors, but also there is something wrong with your puppy.

2. Understand that animals and humans are similar when it comes to needing a variety of different types of vitamins, minerals, and proteins. If we ate the same can of food every day, we probably wouldn't live long, or at least in any state of good health. For the healthiest pooch, you will need to rotate food from different sources.

3. I never feed my own dogs food that contains allergens. While this is a hot topic for humans and their own diets, I have found that dairy, wheat, grains, any nightshade, and potatoes cause severe internal and external chaos with our pooches. Without these allergens, their skin is clear, coats shiny and their minds at ease. When they are reintroduced to these allergens, their skin breaks out in rashes, large pimples

and painful patches of dry skin form. Also, they may also suffer from severe nervous itching, licking, and anxiety.

WARNING

Never feed your dog human food that contains spices, salt, or sugar. These types of foods will also dramatically increase their health problems. Sugar will immediately cause rashes or inflammation of their belly skin and private areas. Those areas will even begin showing signs of moisture similar to yeast or fungal infection.

REGAIN HEALTH

To achieve an optimal diet, all food should be derived from the healthiest sourced food possible. I use a mixture of three different types. For starters, you should divide the food up equally into one dish and mix well. Teacups and Toys can be picky eaters and will dig through their favorite, ignoring the rest. Always check for correct portion sizes listed on the labels of the food packaging.

FEED ADULTS TWO TIMES PER DAY.

FOR PUPPIES, YOU WILL NEED TO FEED MORE
OFTEN, IN SMALLER DOSES.

1. Dry food (extra small bites for puppies)
2. Canned or raw prepared meat (rotation between chicken, bison, venison, beef, lamb, liver and turkey, etc.)
3. Super foods (Raw, Fresh or dehydrated superfood mixture of fruits and vegies)

Dry Food

HOLISTIC CHOICES
There are many different brands of hard dried food on the market today. I would take some time to look for a brand that is natural and grain free.

RUNNY POO
If your doggies poo, is still too soft, increase the dry food until you no longer have that issue. Remember your dog may have a hard time digesting new foods, especially when they are puppies.

Give them plenty of time to get accustomed to their new robust diet before increasing the dry food portion and decreasing the wet.

Canned or Raw Prepared Meet

THE VERY BEST

When it comes to meat, I am looking for the very best and most pure product possible. If you are looking to use raw meat, there are many frozen options available for convenience.

ROTATE

There are so many different meat sources that you can choose from. Because your dog's tummies are fragile you might find that they have trouble digesting one or more of the meats. Feed them slow and watch for their favorite combinations.

Keep a close eye on them after rotating their meat for the first time. They may develop an upset tummy, if it's been a while since the last rotation.

GARBAGE INGREDIENTS

Keep in mind that some dog food brands will fill the meat with unhealthy sugars, such as regular white potatoes or white rice. Avoid these at all cost; they will destroy your dog's health and cause increased vet bills.

Super Foods

MIXING IS EASY

Super foods are an excellent source of nutrients not otherwise found in large quantities in dry or canned food. I usually prepare my super foods by mixing fresh fruits and vegetables that I am already having with my own meal.

NO PREP TIME

If there are left-over salad, veggies or fruit, I will keep them in the refrigerator for the next day. It doesn't take much, so even the smallest left overs are wonderful to use in your dog's food mixture.

GREAT GREENS

Leafy vegetables resemble grasses and other greens that your pooch may eat in the wild. Greens also have numerous health benefits. They are a vitamin powerhouse, full of antioxidants and minerals. They also possess cleansing and pH balancing properties while being an excellent source of fiber.

Examples are lettuces, dandelion leaves, parsley, cilantro, basil, beet tops, carrot tops, kale, sprouted seeds, etc.

DELICIOUS

Sweet vegetables like zucchini, celery, green beans, green peas, red beets, and yams are great toppers. As far as fruits are concerned, my dogs love a few blueberries, papaya, and small chunks of apples with no seeds (apple seeds are toxic to dogs).

SUPER-FOOD BRANDS

Many brands offer super foods fresh or dehydrated for those days you are running short on time. Check your natural food store or online for amazing brands.

PURIFIED WATER

Be sure to use purified or filtered water when possible. There are so many toxins in our city water supply that do great harm to everyone's health including your doggie.

If your puppy or older doggie is having a hard time holding their pee throughout the night, they may be low in salt. Try putting a tiny pinch of Himalayan or Celtic sea salt in their drinking water to help them with maintaining a healthy bladder.

Chapter 11: Toxic Fruits & Vegetables

DEADLY ACCIDENTS

Below is a list of foods that are considered very toxic to your dog. If your pooch has accidently indigested anything on this list, watch them closely for health concerns. Our small dogs have a knack for finding things on the floor that we cannot see, or quickly gobbling something that fell from the counter top. In any event, these reactions can be serious and could cost you a vet visit.

- Grapes & Raisins
- Onions
- Garlic
- Chives
- Cherries
- Mushrooms
- Currants
- Raw & Green Potatoes (exception is the sweet potato)
- Apricot
- Rhubarb
- Apple Seeds
- Tomato Plants
- Avocado in large doses

- Most Nuts

Nightshades Cause Health Problems

BEWARE

The reason why nightshades are problematic for those who consume them is due to the alkaloid content. Consumption of these edible species can be poisonous to anyone, but especially to small animals. These alkaloids are produced by the plants to protect them from harmful insects.

- Bell peppers (a.k.a. sweet peppers)
- Bush tomato
- Cape gooseberry (also known as ground cherries—not to be confused with regular cherries)
- Cocona
- Eggplant
- Garden huckleberry (not to be confused with regular huckleberries)
- Goji berries (a.k.a. wolfberry)
- Hot peppers (chili peppers, jalapenos, habaneros, chili-based spices, red pepper, cayenne)
- Kutjera

- Naranjillas
- Paprika
- Pepinos
- Pimentos
- Regular Potatoes (but not sweet potatoes)
- Tamarillos
- Tomatillos
- Tomatoes

Be sure that you provide your Teacup or Toy with a nutrient rich, allergen and nightshade free diet. With an optimal diet and plenty of exercise, your pooch with live a long healthy life, free of diseases and constant inflammation.

Chapter 12: Dominate Traits

1. Small-breed dogs tend to have a high prey drive. They like to chase after things that run.
2. They show incredible loyalty to their family.
3. They need order, responsibilities and regular tasks (walking, traveling, playing, etc.)
4. They dread being left behind.
5. They have a feast or famine mind-set towards food.
6. They have MORE of an understanding of body language then humans think.
7. They have LESS of an understanding of spoken language then humans think.
8. They have moods, emotion connections, humor and individuality just like humans.
9. They love being nurtured and shown affection.
10. Their body temperature needs to be regulated.

KNOWING YOUR SMALL-BREED

Although they are small lap dogs, teacup and toy breeds still need exercise. Not just to keep them fit, but to stop them from getting bored and destructive.

You will find that when your small-breed reaches adulthood they will require a couple of short walks a day, or a few fifteen-minute play sessions in the back yard. They can be taught to enjoy retrieving games like fetching a ball. This is also a great way to help them blow off steam and let loose.

Brisk walks are wonderful for a healthy pooch, but you will need to build up the distance gradually, so they are not over exhausted keeping up with your longer legs. If you over extend their abilities, their knee can slip out (Luxating Patella).

Also, Teacup and Toy breeds are prone to displaying aggressive behavior towards other dogs, so carefully monitoring their interactions with strange dogs is a must. If you see a large dog coming your way, pick up your doggie to ensure they do not get injured.

Chapter 13: Thinking Like A Dog

SUCCESS IS FUN

The training method used to teach your dog to "stay" will be the same to achieve a bark-free home, along with leash-free walking. During this training, our goal will be to establish a clear line of communication, and eye contact. This will all be made possible by using a treat that your doggie will do anything for.

MISTAKES

The most common mistake I see dog owners do is expecting your dog to understand everything you are saying clearly. While they do understand many things, its primarily centered around body language.

NOTHING IS WORKING

Many dog owners tell me that they scream "no" every time their doggy barks at the door. So, the parents believe that the dog understands that barking is wrong but chooses to do it regardless.

The Observing Dog

You will need to understand how we as humans react to situations before you can truly comprehend and control the behavior of your dog.

Example: Part I

Let's pretend someone just knocked on your door. You immediately go into high alert! You many perk up, turn the radio or television down, giving your total attention to listening for another knock or ring.

You will quickly stand up and move towards the door thinking about who it could be. You carefully peak through the hole or slowly crack the door, trying to see who it is before allowing them in. In some cases, you know exactly who it is, and show excitement when they arrive. These are the physical actions that your dog witnesses and understands.

Reality

While your pooch is very intelligent, it is virtually impossible to establish the right way to act, if they don't understand what they are doing wrong. We will now dive head first into the real reasons why you and your pooch don't communicate well.

Understanding The Dog Mind

Let's say for example, that you are in a foreign country where they speak a different language. You only understand a few words. The words for food, pee, poo, walk, treats and no. However, you do not understand any other words said in the conversation.

Example: Part 2

Now let's pretend that you hear someone at the door. Your friend who only speaks a foreign language yells many words, and periodically you hear the word "no". But the rest is meaningless because you have no idea what they are trying to communicate. Thus, you go ahead and answer the door because someone is knocking.

Even though you understand that "no" is a bad thing, you simply don't know what they are implying, so you answer the door regardless. This is the same situation your pooch is in.

Solving The Language Barrier

I must admit, that cracking the language barrier between you and your dog is one of the most rewarding experiences. When you realize that the power to form a well-behaved dog is in your hands, the relationship dramatically changes. You go from being irritated or outright mad at bad behavior, to sharing a clear meaningful dialog that makes you both happy.

Chapter 14: Your Weapon

SECRETS

The secret to all well-trained dogs comes straight down to providing a reward for their good behavior. They perform - you provide. It's simple!

THERE ARE TWO TYPES OF IMMEDIATE REWARDS

---

1. Edible treats (bits of cooked unseasoned chicken, beef, lamb, pork etc.)
2. Affection (tummy or neck rub, loving words, hugs and kisses)

USE BOTH

Start all dog training by using the treat first and then follow up with affection. This is a sure-fire way to have your dog doing tricks that you didn't even know was possible.

TREATS ARE YOUR SECRET WEAPON

When you begin the training process you will need to have treats galore. Since the treat is your weapon, find the tastiest ones possible that are high quality ingredients. If your pooch seems uninterested in your treats, find better ones.

BEST TRAINING TREATS

The better the treat, the faster they will learn. I like to use a slow baked plain (unseasoned) chicken breast, steak, or lamb. After its cooled, I tear the meat into tiny pieces.

Chapter 15: Fast-Track Training

1. CHALLENGING WORDS

The most challenging words for dogs are the ones that don't link directly to a physical object. You cannot point at a physical object that means "no." Nor can you point at an object that means "quiet." Example words: Inside/outside, stay/come, up/down, bark/quiet, yes/no and so on.

2. EASY WORDS

On the other hand, words like bath, treats, walk, kisses, and car, are easy for dogs to interpret because they have a definite meaning. When you say the word "treats", you shove one in their mouth. When you say "walk", you strap on their harness and go outside. When you say "bath," you put them in warm soapy water.

3. COMBO WORDS

Each challenging word has a combo word that means the opposite. This is where the magic lies. To train your dog not to bark, you will need to teach them the word that means "bark." Then you can teach them the absent of bark which is "quiet." This also works the same with sit/stand, come/stay and many more.

4. ON COMMAND

Focus on the combo word that your dog already knows well. For instance, if they love to bark, start with the command "bark." Then when they understand how to "bark" on command, you can teach them to be "quiet" on command easily.

5. LOOKING FOR APPROVAL

Eye contact demands their attention and respect. If you provide the treat before proper eye contact is made, then they are not asking for your approval.

6. INCREASE INTENSITY

When your pooch is mastering their training, increase the intensity by introducing a distraction. If you're working on "staying," drop a toy and see if they can refuse the urge while keeping eye contact. If you are working on being "quiet," have someone knock on the door one time and increase slowly.

SUCCESS IN BABY STEPS

Don't set them up for failure. Positive reinforcement with a treat is essential. So, go slow and let them show you their new skills.

Creating A Bark-Free Home

TRAINING TAKES REPETITION

Most parents find this method of training to be relaxing. It is fun watching your dog progress in a healthy confident manner. It is also equally amazing that you can do this all on your own, never having to rely on an outside trainer. We all know that when the trainer leaves your pooch reverts to its old ways. This problem arises because the issue stems not only from the dog but the parent as well. You cannot fix one and leave the other broken.

YOU WILL NEED:

- Treats your dog will do anything for (cooled baked chicken, lamb, or beef)
- A quiet room (distractions will be added as the training progresses)

HOW TO BARK ON COMMAND:

1. Sit or kneel in front of your dog.
2. Make sure the treat is ripped into ultra-small pieces.
3. Show them that you have an incredible treat.
4. Say "bark" slowly, and repeat every 30 seconds or so.
5. Do nothing for a long time.........
6. They will perform every trick they can think of; then they will start barking.
7. Say "good," then give them the treat.
8. Repeat the exercise until your dog barks every time you say "bark."

HOW TO BE QUIET ON COMMAND:

1. Sit or kneel in front of your dog.
2. Make sure the treat is ripped into ultra-small pieces.
3. Show them that you have an incredible treat by holding it in front of your face.
4. Say "quiet."

5. The moment they look into your eyes and remain quiet, say "good" and give them the treat.
6. Repeat the exercise until your dog remains "quiet" every time.

MORE CHALLENGING
Now try mixing it up between "bark" and "quiet" until each command is completely understood.

ADD DISTRACTIONS
When you feel very confident in your dog's understanding of each command, it's time to introduce a distraction. This is a great way to test their progress before the situation happens in real life.

SOMEONE IS AT THE DOOR
Try having someone go outside and knock on the door one time. This gives you a distraction that can be managed. When your dog is ready for the next challenge, have the person knock two times.

Continue this exercise until you have full control of your pooch regardless of how many times the person knocks. If this process is taking your pooch longer, spread the training out over days or weeks. It is normal for an older dog to take a bit longer than a puppy.

You Have the Power

From here on out, every time someone comes to the door, your pooch will be waiting for you to indicate the proper behavior. So, make sure you take a moment to glance into their eyes and give them a command.

Sitting

You Will Need:

- Treats your dog will do anything for (cooled baked chicken, lamb, or beef)
- A quiet room (distractions will be added as the training progresses)

Sit on Command:

1. Sit or kneel in front of your dog.
2. Make sure the treat is ripped into ultra-small pieces.
3. Show them that you have an incredible treat by holding it in front of your face.
4. Say "sit."
5. Push their bottom gently to the ground.
6. Say "Good," then give them the treat.

7.   Repeat the exercise until your dog "sits" on their own every time.

ADD DISTRACTIONS

When you feel confident their sitting skills, it's time to introduce a distraction. Use a toy, water bottle, or bone to call their attention away from their sitting position. Continue saying "sit" and demanding their eye contact.

When your pooch has decided to remain sitting, instead of running towards the distraction, reward them with a treat.

Stay

YOU WILL NEED:
*   Treats your dog will do anything for (cooled baked chicken, lamb, or beef)
*   A quiet room (distractions will be added as the training progresses)

STAY ON COMMAND:
1.   This time stand in front of your dog.
2.   Make sure the treat is ripped into ultra-small pieces.
3.   Show them that you have an incredible treat.

4. Say "stay" and at the same time hold out your free hand in a stop position.
5. Lower your hand and slowly take one step back.
6. Come towards your dog, say "good," then give them the treat.
7. Repeat the exercise until your dog "stays" every time.

ADD DISTANCE

When they have mastered the "stay" position at a close range, it's time to move further away.

ADD DISTRACTIONS

When they have mastered the "stay" position at a further range, use a toy, water bottle, or bone to call their attention away. Continue repeating "stay" and demanding their eye contact. When they decide to stay instead of running off, reward them with a treat.

Leash-Free Walking on Command

RUNNING AWAY

Leash free walking is an incredible feeling. Many parents have pooches that will escape from the house or car and run around the neighborhood like a maniac. The fact that these dogs are not afraid of being left behind is a serious issue.

SAFETY FIRST

While many communities and parks require you to have a leash on your pet, knowing that your pooch will follow you everywhere you go is a huge relief. Leash-free walking keeps your pooch from running into roads, yards with pets or children, chasing wild animals, or just running off for good.

YOU WILL NEED:

- Treats your dog will do anything for (cooled baked chicken, lamb, or beef)
- A quiet room (distractions will be added as the training progresses)

LEASH-FREE WALKING AND COME ON COMMAND:

1. Begin the exercise inside your home.
2. Have your dog next to your right leg on the ground.

3.   Make sure the treat is ripped into ultra-small pieces.
4.   Show them that you have their favorite treat.
5.   Begin walking around the house at a slow pace.
6.   As they stay next to you, say "good" and give them a treat.
7.   Continue by increasing the speed and distance.

TIP
When they fall behind, slow down and tell them to "come" while holding out the treat. During this exercise, you will be showing them what the word "come" means. That is why I do not include it under a separate command. This is by far the best way to show them the meaning of this word.

OUTSIDE
When they have mastered following you inside, increase the intensity by letting them follow you in an enclosed outside area. Repeat the exercise until you are confident in their following skills. When the time is right, bring them in a safe open area or trail for additional practice.

Chapter 16: Potty-Training

IT'S GO TIME

I want to quickly begin the potty-training section of this book since your new puppy will be peeing and pooing the moment they get home. If you are reading this book and already have an older Chi that you want to house train, the rules and steps are the same.

SANITATION

Use the wet wipes or a damp rag, to keep your new puppy's bottom area clean.

OUTDOOR TRAINING

If you would like to train a dog to go outside for their bathroom needs, then follow these steps:

1. Taking the puppy outside immediately after meals and upon awaking from a nap or a night's sleep is critical.
2. If you have a fenced back yard, simply bring them outside and allow them time to find a perfect spot.
3. If you do not have a fenced back yard, strap them in their harness and take them for a nice walk.
4. Soon they will realize that either the door or leash allows them to explore and relieve themselves. Watch for your puppy's body language, as they try to communicate their needs with you.

THIS POTTY-TRAINING METHOD IS THE ABSOLUTE BEST

Indoor potty training isn't the easiest thing to do, but you will have long term success and satisfaction. There are other methods/products out there that promise to self-potty-train your doggy with little to no effort. I am here to tell you that there is no such thing available.

If you want the ultimate dog, that pees and poos in the right places, roams the house with no worries, or that can soil on a pee pad in a bathroom stall at the airport. Then you will need to follow my potty-training method exactly.

The Hamper/Box Is Your Savior

REPURPOSED

You and your doggy will soon love this repurposed laundry item. I chose to use the laundry hamper when determining the best method for your new puppy because it only traps them temporarily until they have soiled. You can also substitute the hamper for a sturdy box with taller sides if training an older dog.

Your pooch will initially spend much of its time trying to escape, so make sure the structure can handle the one-sided weight without tipping over.

REWARD WITH ALL YOUR HEART

Your doggy must believe that when they have soiled in the hamper on the pad, not only will they get out, but they will be rewarded.

If for any reason, they think that their potty place is a punishment, they will refuse training. Make sure that your hamper is large and has tall side in comparison to your doggie. Your pooch will need ample room to move around before relieving themselves. Pacing around in circles before peeing or pooing is a natural process.

THINGS THAT DON'T WORK LONG-TERM

I have had many parents use products like the puppy apartment, for potty-training. While it works in the beginning if your puppy is caged; when set free from the apartment, the puppy becomes a peeing-pooing nightmare. It takes much more work to retrain a pooch that has already run amuck, then to do it right the first time.

NIGHT-TIME ACCIDENTS

However, while I do not encourage using a puppy apartment as a training method, I feel that it is an excellent alternative for those parents who sleep very hard throughout the night. While your pooch is young, they will likely need to go at least one time during the night. If you are unable to wake up when they are whimpering, accidents will occur.

By keeping them in a puppy apartment during the night, you can avoid the difficulties of having to retrain them during the day. Once a dog has peed in a specific place, good or bad, they will likely go their again.

YOU WILL NEED

To start, you will need to have a sturdy laundry hamper that has no sharp edges or an equally sturdy box with no top. In addition, you will also need plenty of pee pads. You can find them in most stores and in bulk.

TURNING THE HAMPER INTO A POTTY STATION

Line the inside of the large laundry hamper with a pee pad. It will likely not fit perfect, so fold it until it easily lays at the bottom of the hamper with pad side up.

A Tasty Treat Is Everything

SECRETS

The secret to all well-trained dogs comes straight down to providing a reward for their good behavior. They perform - you provide. It's simple!

TREATS ARE YOUR SECRET WEAPON

When you begin the training process you will need to have treats galore. Since the treat is your weapon, find the tastiest ones possible that are of high quality ingredients. If your pooch seems uninterested in your treats, find better ones.

BEST TRAINING TREATS

The better the treat, the faster they will learn. Again, I like to use a slow baked plain (unseasoned) chicken breast, steak, or lamb. After its cooled, I tear the meat into tiny pieces. This will have your puppy doing tricks you didn't think was even possible.

ON THE ROAD

If you are on the road and you need pocket treats instead, try small bite jerky treats.

Punishment

DON'T DWELL ON ACCIDENTS

Do not punish your pooch for going in the wrong place. If you catch them in the act but cannot make it fast enough to help, then say "no" once, and get your cleaning supplies ready. We want to focus all our efforts on a positive reward-based training method.

ALL THEY WANT

The treats, your attention, and your affection is all your puppy wants. You must offer these things only when they show good behavior and deny them when they are displaying bad behavior. By forcing them to earn your treats, attention, and affection, you will be achieving the highest form of respect.

STEP-BY-STEP INDOOR POTTY TRAINING

Step 1:

THE FIRST STEP TO POTTY-TRAINING IS KNOWING WHEN YOUR POOCH MUST PEE OR POO.

There is only one way to accomplish this task and its easy! You must control their food and water intake. Even though puppies need ample food and water throughout the day, they do not need a heaping bowl to chow on whenever they please. I would not encourage open feeding if potty-training is your goal.

So now that you have a pile of pads, a safe hamper and awesome treats, it's time for the fun to begin. You will start by placing a food and water dish in front of your puppy. After they are done eating, or at least shown no more interest in the food and water, remove it.

FYI: Puppies will need 5 to 30 minutes after eating and drinking before they need to poo or pee.

Step 2:

WATCH THEM LIKE A HAWK FOR SIGNS OF PEE AND POO.

Soon enough your puppy will start to panic and run around in circles sniffing things. This is your sign! the trick to training a puppy to use a pee pad, is by making them use the pad 100% of the time and rewarding them immediately.

Dogs use memory and smell when choosing the perfect place to relieve themselves. Make sure that the hamper is in a place that you would like your puppy to use forever. Placing the pad on a carpeted area is one bad idea. Shoot for a hard surface where slight misses are not going to cause irreparable damage.

Step 3:

QUICKLY PLACE THEM IN THE HAMPER.

When you get the sign, pick them up and place them inside the hamper. They may not go right away. In fact, they could even panic because you are watching them. Either way, continue encouraging your pooch to pee and poo with a soft loving voice the entire time. Avoid touching them during this time even if they are wining to get out.

Step 4:

THEY HAVE SOILED!

The moment they pee or a poo get softly excited, tell them they are good. Then remove them from the hamper and shove a treat in their face. give them a great massage to reaffirm your happiness with their good behavior. You will repeat these steps.

If they are in the hamper for a while and will not go, let them out and continue carefully watching their body language. You many have misjudged their signs and need to wait longer for their food and water to digest.

Step 5:

CLIMBING IN THE HAMPER THEMSELVES.

It won't be long, and your puppy will be trying to get into the hamper themselves. Quickly help them in so they don't have an accident. They will be expecting their treat, so make sure you deliver on the promise. This is such a great sign and moves you closer to a hamper free pee pad. However, you should use the hamper until there is no doubt in your puppy's mind that the hamper is the place to go.

If your puppy begins peeing or pooing on the floor you will need to help them into the hamper right away so that they can see the soil in the right spot and receive the treat. If this is still happening, then you need to go back to watching them more closely.

GETTING RID OF THE HAMPER.

Before you move on to getting rid of the hamper, you should be confident in your puppy's abilities. If they are 100% of the time trying to get into the hamper to pee and poo, then they are ready for a standalone pad.

Step 6:

REMOVE THE HAMPER AND REPLACE WITH PEE PAD HOLDER (HOLDER IS OPTIONAL). OR PLACE DIRECTLY ON THE GROUND.

Now that your puppy is ready to move to the next stage of potty-training, it's time to place the pee pad on top of the pad holder and nix the hamper. The pad holder is entirely optional.

However, sometimes puppies begin to think that all square flat looking rugs are good to relieve themselves on. The pee pad holder helps create a distinct potty area.

Step 7:

CREATING BOUNDARIES

You will see them go over to where they think the hamper should be, but a confused look will cross their face. They may even wait for you to lift them up like you have done before.

Either way, you must help them onto the pad and be ready to create the clear boundaries of each side. You will be using the words "no" to create your boundaries. Basically, you will be creating the sides of the make-believe hamper by saying "no" each time your puppy tries to leave.

EXAMPLE

If they go left trying to step off the pad, you say "no" and gently nudge them back on. If they go right trying to step off the pad you repeat. Soon enough they will succumb to nature and soil the pad. Make sure to immediately congratulate them on their behavior, provide treats and lots of love.

REPEAT

You will need to repeat these steps until your puppy does the routine by themselves.

Roaming the House Freely

ROAM ZONES

Letting your puppy roam freely around the house could be a bit nerve racking. As your puppy grows into a trustworthy adult, this anxiety will fade away. During the puppy stage, you should always use gates to block off certain parts of the house, creating roam zones.

WHY IT'S ESSENTIAL TO ESTABLISH A ROAM ZONE:

- It is much easier for puppies to find their pee pad if it is close by when they realize they need to go. If they are in the laundry room on one end of the house, and their pad is on the other end, they may not be capable of holding it that far.
- The larger the roam zone gets, the more pads you need around. Always have a pad on each level of the home. For those homes that are one level but unusually wide, place a pad at each end.

Using Public Restrooms

LOGICAL SOLUTION FOR A CRAZY IDEA
The thought of having your dog use the public restrooms seems absurd. But for parents of a dog, this is not only a great idea but sometimes a necessity.

NO DOG AREA
I have been to the airport on many occasions where the dog area was on the opposite side. Unfortunately, we don't always have the time or energy to make that long walk. This leaves us in need of a quick place for our dog to pee.

PROBLEM SOLVED
In these types of situations, I just strap on a harness, lay out a pad in a large stall, and encourage my dog to pee or poo.

It can be scary at first for any dog, so make sure that you give them some extra time. If they don't go, try again later, because soon enough they will give into nature and relieve themselves regardless of fear. Be sure always to provide ample rewards and treats to reinforce this good behavior.

Cleaning Up Accidents

SAFETY FIRST
Accidents do occur, and they can range from pee, poo, to vomit. Using the safest products possible is important.

NATURES BEST KEPT SECRETS
I always keep an extra-large box of baking soda around the house. This is a safe and natural cleaner all on its own.

When I discover vomit or anything that is acidic, I will dust it heavily with baking soda. The soda will draw it out of carpet, rugs, upholstery or blankets without bleaching out or damaging the material. This will prevent stains and ensure that the odor is neutralized immediately.

If you are going to use your pet cleaner or a machine spot remover, then just leave the soda for extra cleaning power. When the floor is dry, vacuum the area well to remove baking soda dust.

FYI: Baking soda lifts red liquids right out of the carpet. Heavily dust the fresh stain and wait until it has completely soaked into the soda. Remove the soaked baking soda with paper towels and use a spot cleaner or warm rag to get the rest.

Long-Term Success

GET EXCITED

Make sure that you reward your dog's effort each time they use the pad. Continue offering them treats and loving gestures for the rest of their life. This will ensure long term success.

ADDITIONAL TIPS:

- Keep their poo firm. Diarrhea makes it difficult for your dog to keep their poo on the pad.
- Place a pad down on a hard floor surface. Sometimes your pooch will have lousy aim, or they may have waited too long before dashing to their pad for relief. Either way, it's easier to clean up a mess on a hard surface.
- Carpet holds the smell. Even if you and I cannot smell the urine, a dog can. This presents a challenge when they are deciding where to go,

the pad or the smelly spot. It's truly a tough choice for your pooch.

- Keep soiled pads replaced. After about two pee spots the pad needs to be replaced. If you allow the pad to get too soiled, your dog will go somewhere else. This happens to even the best trained dogs.
- Keep the pad in a private corner. Dogs like to poo in privacy, so make sure that the pad is not out in the open where you commonly gather.
- Use a pee pad holder. For those who use a pee pad holder, their dogs can better differentiate between their pads and a similar size rug.
- Use gates to prevent free roaming of the home. I would suggest using gates to block access off from the entire home, to prevent chewing, trapping, falling, getting stuck and of course peeing and pooing out of site. Keeping your puppy in a smaller area or a single level of the house, will ensure that they can use the pee pad when needed. If they get too far away, then it becomes more difficult to reach in time.
- If your dog hates going poo on the pad, then walk your dog every evening. When going for a walk your dog will automatically desire to poo, resolving this issue altogether.

Chapter 17: Carrier Training

BORN THIS WAY

Since your pooch was born already primed for close companionship, introducing them to a purse or carrier that allows them to go everywhere with you, should not be complicated.

THE RIGHT SIZE

Choosing the right size will come down to how large you believe your new puppy will become as an adult. Since we can roughly estimate that they will be a similar size to the parents you should start there. Many times, the dog carrier description will include weight in addition to length and height. Pull out a measuring tape and try to imagine whether the size is right for you and your puppy.

Some parents choose to purchase a smaller purse/carrier at first and upgrade the bag size as they grow. This is the optimal choice if finances allow.

FIRM BOTTOM

I encourage you to use a carrier that has a stiff or firm bottom. This offers more support and a feeling of safety. Remember that we want our puppy to love this carrier, not feel scared and uncomfortable.

Carrier Training Basics

1. Introducing the carrier. Place the bag on the floor next to your puppy. Get their attention with a yummy treat. Lead them close to the carrier. Give them the treat.
2. Inside. Now try placing the treat inside the carrier (lay down sideways if necessary) letting them get in themselves. Once they are inside, say "inside" and reinforce your happiness with more treats and affection.
3. Outside. Then get their attention with another treat, placing the treat on the floor outside of the carrier, say "outside." Repeat this "inside" and "outside" exercise until it is fully learned.
4. Zip them up. When they have learned that the carrier is good, try zipping it up. Then unzip the bag and give them a treat.
5. Up we go. After your pooch is happily zipped waiting for their next treat, try walking around the house. Then unzip the carrier and give them a treat.
6. New favorite place. Once your puppy has realized that the carrier ensures they will not get left behind, the bag will become one of the most exciting things in their life. A treat all on its own!

Dog Strollers

GAME CHANGER

Having a dog stroller solves many of the challenges that puppy parents face. When taking your pooch shopping at a large department store, you may have trouble carrying everything. By using a stroller, not only will it free up one arm, but it also provides an easy place to store extra bags, coats, and your pooch.

If you are going to the park, take your stroller. You can pack yourself a lunch and something to drink with the extra space.

WALKING TOO MUCH

Many small-breeds will eventually develop significant hip, knee and joint problems in their old age. These issues are intensified when your pooch is overweight, eating inflammatory foods, and not adequately hydrated.

Since these breeds are born with these underlying genetic issues, over exercising their painful joints can cause further damage. Therefore, when you desire that long stroll in the neighborhood, countryside or park; take the stroller and let them hitch a ride when they are getting tired.

Chapter 18: Crates and Cages

There are many reasons for crating or caging your pooch.

1.   You are a hard sleeper and cannot help your puppy use the bathroom during the night.

2. You work long hours and are not 100% confident that they will use the pee pad during the entire day.
3. You have friends and family over, and you are not able to provide close supervision during your puppy's potty-training.

If you are going to use a crate, be sure to exercise your doggy before caging. Also, provide plenty of bones or chew toys, so they don't sit idle and become extremely bored. Some parents experience heavy yapping during crating time in the absence of toys and bones.

LOVING THE CRATE

Before you shove your dog in the crate and close the door, follow the same steps of carrier training in Secret #17. Use plenty of treats to help them freely get in and out of the crate.

After a trusting atmosphere is formed between doggy and crate, try closing and opening the door while offering more treats. Your goal is to make this a super fun and relaxing place to be. Avoid creating stress towards the crate.

Alternatives to Crating/Caging

BRING THEM EVERYWHERE

Your Chi is wired genetically to desire full-time companionship. They love to be on your lap, in your arms, by your side, in your bed, in the car or being carried. The best way to get your puppy comfortable with traveling is taking them everywhere from the start.

Instead of crating them at home, bring them to work. Don't leave them behind when they can ride along in the car and wait for you to buy groceries. If you bring them along from a young age, you will develope an amazing loyal companion.

STEPPING STOOL

When your dog is potty-trained, invest in a reliable stepping stool to get on and off your bed. This way they can use the bathroom without ever having to bother you during the night.
You could also place a stepping stool against the sofa, so they can avoid jumping down from high places. Over time this could prevent significant joint damage.

I JUST WANT TO WATCH

If you are in the kitchen, find a safe place for them to sit and quietly observe. If you need to use the restroom, bring them. If you have friends or family over and need to attend to other things, let someone else hold your new baby. Handling them often is a great exercise, and they love it.

Chapter 19: Toxins Can Kill

POISONS EVERYWHERE

There are so many toxins in dog food, flea and tick treatments, vaccinations, unpurified water, yard sprays and fertilizers and the list go on. Our Teacup and Toy dogs are not equipped to handle these potentially fatal doses of chemicals and neurotoxins.

HIGHEST RATES

Small-breed dogs less than 10 pounds, have the highest rate of reaction to the ingredients in common products found in our stores and environment. Many parents have witnessed serious medical conditions and deaths with their own doggies. Learning to avoid these deadly chemicals is much easier than trying to cure the diseases they create.

OVERWHELMING SUPPORT

I received such a strong reaction to this topic when talking amongst the small-breed dog community. They shared stories that broke my heart into a million pieces.

I had an overwhelming request to include all of the homeopathic dog remedies that I personal use.

However, before I move onto the natural remedies, we must uncover products and overlooked places that our tiny dogs can easily become exposed to deadly toxins.

Chapter 20: Flea and Tick Treatments

There are deadly ingredients found in top-brand flea and tick treatments. While you will likely need flea and tick treatments for your new puppy, there are better natural alternative that you can make yourself or purchase. Below I have listed the most harmful chemicals that will compromise your dog's immune system and overall health.

FIPRONIL

The EPA's Pesticide Division found that the active ingredient Fipronil (in most top brands) remains in a pet's system with the potential for nervous system and thyroid toxicity.

Laboratory animal test resulted in thyroid cancer and altered thyroid hormones, liver and kidney toxicity, reduced fertility and convulsions.

IMIDACLOPRID

In lab studies, Imidacloprid has been found to increase cholesterol levels in dogs, cause thyroid lesions, create liver toxicity. It also has the potential to damage the liver, heart, lungs, spleen, adrenals, brain, and gonads.

This dangerous neurotoxin can cause incoordination along with labored breathing and muscle weakness. Imidacloprid is readily found in Advantage and other top brands.

When this drug was tested after its introduction in 1994, researchers found an increase in the frequency of birth defects. In the Journal of Pesticide Reform, thyroid lesions are a result of exposure to imidacloprid.

PYRETHRINS

It has been a misconception that Pyrethrins (naturally occurring compounds from the chrysanthemum plant) and pyrethroids (the synthetic counterpart) are less hazardous than other ingredients.

But pyrethroid-based insecticides was causing double the fatalities in our dogs than that of other flea treatments without this ingredient.

Pyrethroid also accounted for more than half of the "more serious" pesticide reactions including brain damage, heart attacks and seizures.

PERMETHRIN AND/OR PYRIPROXYFEN

Bio Spot Flea and Tick Control, Defend EXspot Treatment and Zodiac FleaTrol Spot On, all contain either or both of the active ingredients Permethrin and/or Pyriproxyfen.

Permethrin is a carcinogenic insecticide. This ingredient causes lung cancer and liver tumors in lab animals. It can also act as a neurotoxin, causing tremors as well as increased aggressive behavior and learning difficulties. This is a substitute ingredient for brands looking to escape the negative publicity of the other more common ingredients.

KILLERS

These ingredients are alarming and should never be put on your precious puppies!

In later chapters, I have compiled some incredible DIY flea and tick remedies for you to use and share.

Chapter 21: Vaccinations and Chart

CRAZY SCIENCE

Most vaccines are prescribed on a 1-dose-fits-all basis, rather than by body weight. This concept is especially alarming when we are discussing the effects of large doses on our tiny puppies.

SMALL VS. LARGE

A Chi and an adult Great Dane are commonly given the same dose in each shot. They get the same volume of virus or bacteria plus the same volume of adjuvants (like aluminum), preservatives (like mercury), antibiotics, stabilizers and foreign tissue cultures (like fetal calf serum). All these ingredients are known to cause vaccine reactions.

REACTION TIMES

Vaccine reactions can occur within minutes or days. I have listed some of the signs you must watch for after your dog has received any vaccinations. Take the time to review the best options with your veterinarian.

- urticaria (hives)
- whole-body soreness (muscle or joint aches)
- angioedema (tissue swelling)

- emesis (vomit)
- diarrhea
- hypotension (low blood pressure)
- anorexia (decreased appetite)
- ataxia (stumbling)
- collapse
- coma
- death

Talk to your doctor about giving your new puppy size related doses. Alos, you can now purchase and self-administer all recommended vaccinations if you choose.

Below are all vaccination recommendations, length of immunity, and who needs them. Also, included is the age your puppy should be when they are administered. If you are self-administering, be sure to document the vaccinations thoroughly. This document will be needed for almost all groomers, airlines, and boarding facilities.

AVMA Vaccination Recommendations

Component	Class	Efficacy	Length of Immunity	Comments
Canine Distemper	Core	High	> 1 year for	
Measles	Noncore	High in preventing disease, but not in preventing infection	Long	Use in high risk environments for canine distemper in puppies 4-10 weeks of age
Parvovirus	Core	High	> 1 year	
Hepatitis	Core	High	> 1 year	Only use canine adenovirus-2 (CAV-2) vaccines
Rabies	Core	High	Dependent upon type of vaccine	
Respiratory disease from canine adenovirus-2 (CAV-2)	Noncore	Not adequately studied	Short	
Parainfluenza	Noncore	Intranasal MLV - Moderate Injectable MLV - Low	Moderate	Only recommended for dogs in kennels, shelters, shows, or large colonies; If vaccination warranted, boost annually or more frequently
Bordetella	Noncore	Intranasal MLV - Moderate Injectable MLV - Low	Short	For the most benefit, use intranasal vaccine 2 weeks prior to exposure
Leptospirosis	Noncore	Variable	Short	Up to 30% of dogs may not respond to vaccine
Coronavirus	Noncore	Low	Short	Risk of exposure high in kennels, shelters, shows, breeding facilities
Lyme	Noncore	Appears to be limited to previously unexposed dogs; variable	Revaccinate annually	

DOG VACCINATION SCHEDULE BY WEEKS

Dog Vaccination Schedule	
Age	**Vaccination**
5 weeks	**Parvovirus**: for puppies at high risk of exposure to parvo, some veterinarians recommend vaccinating at 5 weeks. Check with your veterinarian.
6 & 9 weeks	**Combination vaccine*** without leptospirosis. Coronavirus: where coronavirus is a concern.
12 weeks or older	**Rabies**: Given by your local veterinarian (age at vaccination may vary according to local law).
12 & 15 weeks**	**Combination vaccine** **Leptospirosis**: include leptospirosis in the combination vaccine where leptospirosis is a concern, or if traveling to an area where it occurs. **Coronavirus**: where coronavirus is a concern. **Lyme**: where Lyme disease is a concern or if traveling to an area where it occurs.
Adult (boosters)§	**Combination vaccine** **Leptospirosis**: include leptospirosis in the combination vaccine where leptospirosis is a concern, or if traveling to an area where it occurs. **Coronavirus**: where coronavirus is a concern. **Lyme**: where Lyme disease is a concern or if traveling to an area where it occurs. **Rabies**: Given by your local veterinarian (time interval between vaccinations may vary according to local law).

Chapter 22: The Lawn Chemicals

THE SICKNESS IS IN THE GRASS

This is an area of risk that most pet owners generally overlook. However, since we are parents to a very small dog breed, this becomes even more important. The pesticides and fertilizers used in lawn care, are absolutely one of the most dangerous places for our Teacup and Toys to playing.

WHEN WALKING YOUR DOG TURNS DEADLY

Think about when you are walking your doggie around the neighborhood or park. We let our pooches skim across every piece of grass.

In a perfect world, this would be the best things that you could do for your dog. However, each patch of grass or edging of the street has typically been sprayed with deadly chemicals.

PUBLIC HAZARD
In fact, public and city properties along with larger gated communities pay to have a special service that handles routine spray of these health hazard poisons. If you are lucky they will put up signs up to notify you of the contamination. But if you are like most, you will have no idea.

SPRAYING FRENZY
These chemicals are sprayed all over your parks, neighborhoods, streets, edging, gardens and more. When it rains, and your pooch drinks the water off the concrete, they are likely drinking run-off poisons.

Lawn Chemicals That Kill

EXPOSURE
I have included common ingredients of Lawn Pesticides, and some of the signs to watch for. If you believe that your lawn, or the lawn of others is contaminated, stop the exposure immediately. Make sure to bath your doggie to remove any harmful residue from the skin and paw area.

Organophosphates

These compounds include some of the most toxic chemicals used in agriculture. They are fat-soluble and easily be transmitted throughout the skin. Examples are Chloryprifos and Diazinon.

SYMPTOMS INCLUDE:
- excessive salivation
- moist respiratory sounds
- vomiting
- diarrhea
- slow heart rates
- abdominal pain
- pinpointed pupils

Carbamates

These are similar to organophosphates. They inhibit the same enzyme pathway. This also includes the commonly used insecticide Carbamyl.

EXPOSURE CAUSES:
- convulsions
- dizziness

- labored breathing
- nausea, vomiting
- diarrhea
- unconsciousness
- muscle cramps
- excessive salivation

Phenoxy and Benzoic Acid Herbicides

These herbicides like 2,4 D, MCPP, and MCPA affect the central nervous system. Dogs don't excrete acids as efficiently as humans and are highly sensitive to this chemical. An EPA-funded study concluded that 2,4-D is easily tracked indoors, exposing children and pets at levels ten times higher than pre-application levels. Exposure to phenoxy-treated lawns and gardens appeared to increase the risk of bladder cancer.

SOME SYMPTOMS INCLUDE:
- involuntary twitching
- loss of sensation
- vomiting, diarrhea
- weakness
- stomach pains

- fatigue
- dermatitis
- sore muscles

Pyrethroids

These compounds affect the central and peripheral nervous systems. Permethrin and Resmethrin compounds are regularily used in this group.

SYMPTOMS INCLUDE:
- muscle tremors
- hyperexcitability
- depression
- ataxia
- vomiting
- seizures
- anorexia
- death

Organochlorines

These are a well-known toxic and compounds such as PCBs, PCE, and DDT.

Death is caused by respiratory failure during seizures and also a high body temperature. Long-term exposure increases neurological damage, respiratory illness, and many types of cancers. While the US is trying to regulate the deadly chemical

Organochlorine, it is still used in seed-coating agents. Also, you can find it as an active ingredient in medicated shampoos for lice and scabies.

SYMPTOMS INCLUDE:
- muscle tremors
- twitches
- respiratory problems
- seizures

STOP DEADLY LAWN CHEMICALS

FEEL GOOD

Use only natural and organic products in your own lawn, so that you can feel good about letting your pooch frolic freely. Here are some extra tips below that will help you create the safest environment for your pooch, yourself, and loved ones.

FOLLOW THE FIVE EASY STEPS:

1. Adjust the pH so that your soil is at peak pH for grass to grow (around 6.5).
2. Use organic pesticides and slow-release fertilizer.
3. Use homeopathic or home-made remedies for ants and spiders.
4. Over-seed to encourage more grass to grow. Spread seed especially in the spring and fall.
5. Mow High (around 3 inches) to crowd out the weeds.

GET ACTIVE!

Spread the word about safer alternatives by putting "pesticide free" lawn signs in your yard.

Chapter 23: Poisonous House Plants

HARMFUL OR HARMLESS
All the plants on this list are commonly found in homes. However, this is not a complete list only the most common. If you have houseplants that are not on this list, visit www.Aspca.org to ensure they are non-poisonous.

OUT OF REACH
If you have a few of these plants at home, then move them entirely out of reach from your doggie.

- Aloe Vera
- Hedera Helix "Ivy"
- Crassula Ovata "Jade"
- Dieffenbachia "Dumb Cane"
- Philodendron
- Epipremnum Aureum "Pothos," also known as "Devil's Ivy"
- Cycas Revoluta "Sago Palm"
- Zamioculcas "ZZ Plant"
- Caladium "Elephant Ear"
- Dracaena Fragrans "Corn Plant"
- Asparagus Fern
- Lilies (except Easter and Stargazer lilies)

- Ferns (except Boston Fern)

Chapter 24: Natural Solutions to Health Issues

A GIFT OF HEALTH

There are so many medications and topical solutions for your doggie. However, most of them will include toxins that will rapidly deteriorate your dog's health. I have included all the homeopathic remedies I use on my own dogs. I hope you and your new companion enjoy these for years to come.

PREVENT:
- Tear Eyes
- Fleas

- Ticks
- Ants
- Spiders
- Parasites
- and more…

Tear Eyes

IT'S NOT YOUR PUPPIES FAULT

Wet tearing eyes are usually a sign of a poor allergen laced diet. Most breeders will have their dogs on diets plum full of allergens. They also contain a plethora of dyes, sugars and strange chemicals causing inflammation.

Sugar is your pooch's worst nightmare. It causes and or allows fungus and yeast to grow ramped. If something is moist and smells funny anywhere on your dog, then you have a sugar problem.

BAD WATER

Tear staining may be further compounded by bad water. Switch your puppy to a purified water source.

TEETHING

Puppies tend to have worse tear staining when they are teething. Since this is a temporary stage it will lesson in time.

ENVIRONMENT
Tear stains can also be worsened by a dusty or smoky environment.

DOCTORED PHOTOS
It is very typical for puppies to have some eye stains. For those who are purchasing (or have) purchased online, many times breeders will touch up the photos so that we cannot see the obvious. For those who have, or will see the puppy prior to purchasing, a good bath and eye stain wash can also fool you.

SOLUTIONS
Either way, I wouldn't stress about it. There are plenty of natural tear stain solutions and cleaners in every pet store or online. Make sure that you are paying special attention to their diet and the problem should solve itself without any extra help

Wipe Out Worms

A NON-TOXIC SOLUTION

Conventional wormers are chemical-based pesticides, containing carcinogens and toxins that are harmful. These chemicals build up in your doggy's system over time, causing internal damage. Fortunately, there are so many natural ways to remove worms. There are also companies that specialize in providing homeopathic medicines for dogs.

WORMS ARE EVERYWHERE

Many parents have a misconception that dogs either have worms or they don't. While this could be true at any given moment, dogs come in contact with worms on a regular basis. Most worms die before becoming an issue if your pooch's immune system is running at optimal speed. With that being said, worms should be viewed as something that must constantly be managed through diet and preventive measures.

CARING CURES

I have provided a handy list of local whole foods that can be administered on a regular basis to prevent and manage worms. Although I am focusing on our pets, these foods are also wonderful for our own management of parasites. Use the following remedies below on a daily basis if you know your pooch has a worm infestation. If not, then try incorporating them into their diet weekly for optimal worm prevention.

PUMPKIN SEEDS

These tasty snacks are the most potent and effective curative agent against tapeworm and hookworm. Scientific studies have shown that pumpkin seed elements are effective in eliminating these worms in both human and animals. Cucurbitacin, an amino acid in the pumpkin seed eliminates the parasites from the dog's belly and at the same time providing a rich source of zinc, calcium, potassium, niacin and Vitamin A.

HOW TO USE:

Use a grinder to grind the raw or sprouted pumpkin seeds into a powder. Mix ½ teaspoon to every 5 pounds of your dog's weight in their food daily. If using only as a preventative measure, try adding to their food one time per week.

CLOVES

Cloves have been used by ancient cultures to treat parasites in both humans and animals and is often found in anti-parasitic mixtures.

HOW TO USE:

Provide ½ of a clove per day for one week for every 5 pound of dog weight. This could be ground and mixed in the food or whole. After this, every other week for the next two months. By then, parasites would have been expelled from your dog.

OREGON GRAPE ROOT

The medicinal properties come from the roots of the plant, not the berries. The plant contains berberine a substance that boosts the immune system, rids infections and act as an antiseptic. It is effective against viruses, bacteria, fungi, and parasites. The plant also is used to cleanse and support the liver.

HOW TO USE:

The medicinal properties of Oregon grape are best used by tincture. Three drops to 5 pounds of dog weight, twice per day for one week. Do not medicate pregnant dogs and those with liver problems. Use only if your pooch currently has a worm infestation. Try the other whole food methods listed in this section for prevention.

TURMERIC

This spice has anti-parasitic properties and creates an environment that is not conducive to the growth of worms. Turmeric also heals the areas of the intestines were worm infestation occurs.

HOW TO USE:
Provide 1/8 tsp of fresh grated turmeric per day, for every 5 pounds of dog weight. Make sure your dog has lots of fresh water to ensure that they don't get constipated. Turmeric powder is just fine to use if you cannot find the fresh root. This root looks like ginger but is orange instead. Cut the outside skin off and shred the root over a any fine grater.

PAPAYA

Papaya is an excellent source of digestive enzymes that carry out protein digestion of parasites.

HOW TO USE:

Look for a mature green papaya in the nearest food store. Dice fruit into bite sized chunks and add a small amount to your doggy's food. If they digest it well then you can add a little more to their next meal. This is also a great superfood to add to their regular diet.

DIATOMACEOUS EARTH

Diatomaceous earth is a white powdery substance that is made from fossilized remains of small water creatures.

HOW TO USE:

Only ensure that you select the one labeled as food grade. Smaller dogs can get one 1/4 of a teaspoon daily. Always mix the substance thoroughly in the dog's meal so they do not inhale it accidently. Use only if your pooch currently has a worm infestation. Try the other whole food methods listed in this section for regular prevention.

CARROTS

Carrots are a safe source of nutrients and great support for your dog's immune system. Also, excellent for using in combination with raw pumpkin seed powder, Oregon grape, turmeric, papaya or clove.

HOW TO USE:
Add coarsely chopped carrots to your dogs food. Carrots act as roughage as it goes through the gut. It will scrape all mucus from the walls of the stomach and intestines bringing with it all parasites that are lodged. This is also a great superfood to add to their regular diet.

Safe Ant & Spider Spray

MUST HAVE
My go to ant and spider problem solver, is a classic peppermint spray remedy. This mixture will keep ants and spiders out of your home and yard with absolutely no chemicals or toxins!

VICTORY

Most bugs, especially ants and spiders, despise the smell of peppermint. It doesn't kill them, they just hate it with a passion and stay away at all cost. That is why I am such a huge fan of this remedy. I keep the bugs away and they get to keep their life. It is a win-win for everyone.

VERSATILE

Spray it around the insides of your doors and windows, or anywhere you believe the critters are getting in. You can also spray a little near your dogs water or food dishes. This is a great spray for the patio, grilling and pool area. Everyone will love the incredible smell of the peppermint.

ANT HILLS

Place a few drops of Peppermint Essential Oil in the opening of the ant hill and they will hit the road!

INGREDIENTS:

- 1 small spray bottle
- Distilled water
- 2 tablespoons of witch hazel
- 12 drops of Peppermint Essential Oil

DIRECTIONS:

Take your small spray bottle and fill it 3/4 full of distilled water. Add 2 tablespoons of witch hazel to the spray bottle. Then add 12 drops of Peppermint Essential Oil. Shake it well and spray away!

Flea Remedies

KILL FLEAS WITH EASE

There are so many wonderful non-toxic remedies that you can use, as well as natural store-bought formulas to fight fleas. As I have previously mentioned the toxins found in common flea and tick medications are deadly to our puppies.

10 FLEA FACTS:

1. A flea can drink 15 times its weight in blood in just a single day!
2. Scientists have found over 2,000 types of fleas and continue to find different ones each year!
3. The biggest flea that has been found measured in at about 2.5cm!
4. Scientists have shown that fleas can jump up to 8 inches!
5. Fleas have been known to live for two years after having just a single meal of blood!

6.   For every flea that you find in your home, there are statistically about 80 others hidden from your sight!
7.   Pets with fleas can develop anemia and tapeworms.
8.   Research shows that fleas have been around for over 165 million years!
9.   Humans can get fleas and suffer from small sores and allergies.
10. Fleas live in moist shaded areas (overgrown bushes or shrubbery)

Home-Made Flea Collar

A flea collar is a great way to ward off fleas and is free of all toxins.

INGREDIENTS:
- 3-5 drops of cedar oil or lavender oil
- 1-3 tablespoons of water
- Bandana OR your dog's collar
- Eyedropper (optional)

DIRECTIONS:

Dilute 2-3 drops of your chosen oil in 1-3 tablespoons of water. Apply 5-10 drops of the mixture the bandana or collar and rub the sides of the fabric together. Reapply oil mixture to the collar once a week. In conjunction with this, 1 or 2 drops of oil diluted with at least 1 tablespoon of olive oil can be placed at the base of your dog's tail.

Flea Deterring Drink

I love using this flea deterring drink for my doggies. They don't mind the vinegar, and I feel much better about them running around the yard or playing with other dogs.

INGREDIENTS:

- 1 teaspoon white distilled vinegar or apple cider vinegar
- Purified Water

DIRECTIONS:

For every 5-pound dog add 1/8 teaspoon of white distilled vinegar or apple cider vinegar to ½ cup drinking water. I highly recommend using Braggs Apple Cider Vinegar. This solution will improve skin and coat condition from the inside-out.

Flea Spray

This flea spray is an easy way to prevent fleas as well as ticks from hitching a ride on your pooch. It also makes their hair shimmer for days on end.

INGREDIENTS:
- 1 cup apple cider vinegar
- 1-quart fresh water
- 2-3 drops of lavender or cedar oil
- 1 medium/large sized spray bottle

DIRECTIONS:
Add 2-3 drops of oil with 1 cup of apple cider vinegar. Then mix with 1 quart of fresh water. Fill your spray bottle, and mist your dog. Do not spray directly at their face. To get around the neck and behind the ears, dampen a soft cloth with the mixture and wipe it on. Lightly spray their bedding and resting areas.

Flea Bath

Wash your pooch to kill fleas on the spot.

INGREDIENTS:
- 1/2 cup of freshly squeezed lemon juice
- 1 ½ – 2 cups of fresh water

- 1/4 –1/2 cup of shampoo (plant based - natural for dogs)

DIRECTIONS:

Stir together lemon juice, water, and pet shampoo. Bottle the remainder and use every few days until fleas are gone. Make sure that you message the mixture deep into the hair and rinse thoroughly.

Amber Resin Collars

REPELS BUGS NATURALLY

Baltic amber resin collars for flea and tick prevention is a wonderful product and is super cute. Amber is a resin that formed millions of years ago. It has electrostatic properties that repels fleas and ticks. Amber also has a unique smell and a beautiful appearance.

WHAT TO LOOK FOR

The amber must be raw and unpolished. Electrostatic electricity makes it impossible for fleas, ticks, and other bugs to remain on your pet's coat.

The raw amber has healing qualities for animals as well as humans. When shopping, look for raw high-quality resin stones, strong collars, and the ability to create your own collar size based on actual neck measurements.

Chapter 25: Let Them Be a Hero

Teach your doggie at least one fun trick that will amaze your friends and family.

Everyone cheers in amazement when the dog in the commercial fetches a beer from the refrigerator during the ball game. Let your dog be that hero that everyone falls in love with.

If you commonly misplace your television remote control, teach your dog to find it for you. The steps are simple.

1. Show them the remote and give him a treat.
2. Set the remote down, tell them to find it, and if they even look at the remote, give them a treat.
3. When they locate the remote on command every time, hide it. Just hide it simple at first, then make it more complicated as you go.

Your dog's fantastic nose will lead them to the remote every time, much to everyone's amazement. small-breed dogs are excellent entertainers, so this will likely become their favorite game.

If you don't have trouble locating your remote control, teach them to find things such as your keys or wallet.

CONGRATULATIONS
Teacup and Toy breeds are a gift to their doting parents. Your new puppy will be the highlight of your family and home for years to come. They will provide you with an incredible companionship that cannot be duplicated by another animal ever again.

BEING THE BEST PARENT
Being a parent to a small-breed isn't always the easiest. None the less, you are doing so with enthusiasm and great love. The secrets found in these pages will arm you with the knowledge you need to provide the best training and care possible. You can now quickly be on your way to creating a healthy, well behaved doggie.